DODD, MEAD WONDERS BOOKS include WONDERS OF:

ALLIGATORS AND CROCODILES. Blassingame
ANIMAL NURSERIES. Berrill
BARNACLES. Ross and Emerson
BAT WORLD. Lavine
BEYOND THE SOLAR SYSTEM. Feravolo
BISON WORLD. Lavine and Scuro
CACTUS WORLD. Lavine
CAMELS. Lavine
CARIBOU. Rearden
CORALS AND CORAL REEFS. Jacobson and Franz
CROWS. Blassingame
DINOSAUR WORLD. Matthews
DONKEYS. Lavine and Scuro
EAGLE WORLD. Lavine
ELEPHANTS. Lavine and Scuro
FLY WORLD. Lavine
FROGS AND TOADS. Blassingame
GEESE AND SWANS. Fegely
GEMS. Pearl
GOATS. Lavine and Scuro
GRAVITY. Feravolo
HAWK WORLD. Lavine
HERBS. Lavine
HOW ANIMALS LEARN. Berrill
HUMMINGBIRDS. Simon
JELLYFISH. Jacobson and Franz
KELP FOREST. Brown
LLAMAS. Perry
LIONS. Schaller
MARSUPIALS. Lavine
MEASUREMENT. Lieberg
MONKEY WORLD. Berrill
MOSQUITO WORLD. Ault
OWL WORLD. Lavine
PELICAN WORLD. Cook and Schreiber
PONIES. Lavine and Casey
PRAIRIE DOGS. Chace
PRONGHORN. Chace
RACCOONS. Blassingame
RATTLESNAKES. Chace
ROCKS AND MINERALS. Pearl
SEA GULLS. Schreiber
SEA HORSES. Brown
SEALS AND SEA LIONS. Brown
SNAILS AND SLUGS. Jacobson and Franz
SPIDER WORLD. Lavine
SPONGES. Jacobson and Pang
STARFISH. Jacobson and Emerson
STORKS. Kahl
TERNS. Schreiber
TERRARIUMS. Lavine
TREE WORLD. Cosgrove
TURTLE WORLD. Blassingame
WILD DUCKS. Fegely
WOODS AND DESERT AT NIGHT. Berrill
WORLD OF THE ALBATROSS. Fisher
WORLD OF BEARS. Bailey
WORLD OF HORSES. Lavine and Casey
WORLD OF SHELLS. Jacobson and Emerson
WORLD OF WOLVES. Berrill
YOUR SENSES. Cosgrove

Wonders of Ponies

Sigmund A. Lavine and Brigid Casey

Illustrated with photographs and old prints

DODD, MEAD & COMPANY   NEW YORK

TO GERT

AND

TO DENNIS

AND

TO OUR MUTUAL EDITOR

ILLUSTRATIONS COURTESY OF: The British Tourist Authority, 32, 71; Michael T. Casey, 27, 62; Dartmoor Pony Society, Corscombe, Dorset, 35; Linda Denegar, 3, 8, 9, 14, 16 *right*, 23, 26, 33, 64 *left*, 76 *top and bottom*; Exmoor Pony Society, Williton, Somerset, 34; Walter Genbrugge/Photo Trends, 21; Elizabeth Gingell, Master, Cambridgeshire Harriers, 31; Irish Tourist Board, 11, 28, 52; Tina Krettecos, 12, 53; Ted Lewin, 45; Jane Latta/Photo Trends, 48; National Foundation Happy Horsemanship for Handicapped, Inc., Malvern, Pa., 78; Pamela Nelson, 30; New Forest Pony Breeding and Cattle Society, Ringwood, Hants., 37; Pony of the Americas Club, Inc., Mason City, Iowa, 39, 58, 60; Sam Savitt, 38, 43, 67; Alexander Turnbull Library, Wellington, 75; Vincent Scuro, 13, 15, 16 *left*, 54; Somerset Hills Handicapped Riders Club, Bedminster, N.J., photo by Linda Diana Bohm, 79; Salem Tamer, 76 *left; The Times*/Photo Trends, 41; Welsh Pony Society of America, Winchester, Va., 55.

Title page: Tennessee Walking Horse pony

Copyright © 1980 by Sigmund A. Lavine and Brigid Casey
All rights reserved
No part of this book may be reproduced in any form
without permission in writing from the publisher
Printed in the United States of America

1 2 3 4 5 6 7 8 9 10

Library of Congress Cataloging in Publication Data

Lavine, Sigmund A
Wonders of ponies.

Includes index.
SUMMARY: Discusses the characteristics, history, breeds, lore, and uses of ponies.
1. Ponies—Juvenile literature. [1. Ponies]
I. Casey, Brigid, joint author. II. Title.
SF315.L38   636.1'6   79-6643
ISBN 0-396-07814-1

Contents

1. Why Isn't a Pony a Horse? — 7
2. Pony Characteristics — 10
3. History of the Pony — 18
4. Pony Breeds — 25
5. Pony Lore — 49
6. When Is a Pony Not a Pony? — 56
7. Pony Potpourri — 63
8. Uses of Ponies — 69
   Index — 80

Street photographers and their ponies were once a common sight in New York and other large cities. Many of these photos are treasured family keepsakes. Here two generations of one family are pictured with photographers' ponies, their faces mirroring the joy and wonder of associating with a horse. The boy on the left was photographed in the late 1920's in Brooklyn; his daughter below in 1954 and 1956 in Manhattan.

1 Why Isn't a Pony a Horse?

What is a pony?

A pony can be many things. To a child it might be a little circus horse with tall plumes on its head, a beloved pet—or a dream horse, perhaps a Mustang racing across the prairie to freedom.

A pony can be many things to an adult, too—a means of making a living, or the source of pleasure-filled hours of riding. To horse lovers of all ages, a pony is a wild spirit that has galloped into the hearts of man.

Horsemen are engaged in a never ending dispute over what the word "pony" really means. One reason is the fact that years ago all horses were the size of ponies. Today breeders of certain small horses insist their animals are *not* ponies, while other breeders who raise ponies maintain that their small stock is *not* composed of horses. The arguments advanced by both groups have merit. As a result, a number of hippologists—students of the horse—are convinced that it is impossible to answer the question "What is a pony?" accurately.

Therefore, horse fanciers have accepted a compromise—a

rule that decrees that any horse fifty-eight inches or less in height is to be classified as a pony. To determine this height, the distance from the ground to the top of the withers (the highest part of the shoulders) is measured. The average pony stands between forty and fifty inches at the shoulder. Ponies thirty-two inches or less are classified as midgets.

Although breeders often give a pony's height in inches, the traditional unit of measure for equines is the hand. Like the digit and the foot, the term "hand" originated with primitive man who employed units of length that matched parts of the body. In all probability, a hand—the equivalent of four inches—represents the width of some early tribal leader's palm.

When the owner of a pony says it stands "twelve-two," he means the animal is twelve hands, two inches tall. Expressed in inches, the pony measures fifty (four times twelve, plus two).

Incidentally, individual Quarter Horses and Thoroughbreds

This grade pony's owner bought him at a livestock sale for $57.00 and has little idea of his breeding. But he says Deranged Richard is the best pony he ever drove, often winning in halter classes as well.

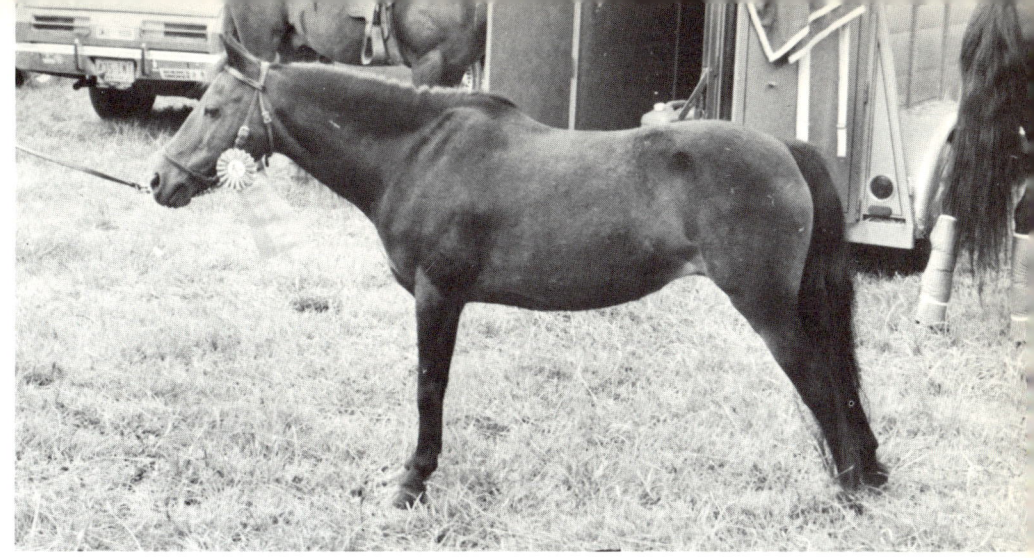

Shetland Crescent's Debutante, seventeen, won the New York State Saddle Horse Association's trophy for pleasure driving pony of 1978.

may stand under 14.2—fifty-eight inches—which is lower than their breed's normal height. Nor is it uncommon for Morgan and Arabian horses to be pony sized. Such animals can be entered in either horse or pony classes at shows.

Purebred vs. Grade

A pony is either a purebred or the result of mixed breeding. To be classified as a purebred, all of a pony's ancestors not only have to be of the same breed but also must have been registered (officially recorded in a breed studbook).

Grade ponies—those with mixed ancestry—cannot be registered. Nevertheless, over the centuries, countless ponies of undeterminable breeding have been the delight of young riders and the helpful companions of farmers, lumbermen, and miners. Although grade ponies make charming pets and can be willing and energetic workers, they are vanishing despite the fact that they cost less than registered stock. Perhaps the most important reason for the decline of the grade pony's popularity is the increasing interest in showing and racing registered ponies.

2 Pony Characteristics

Ponies, like people, are individuals. Thus ponies vary in disposition and differ in manners. While some breeds are considered more suitable for younger horsemen than others, the majority of ponies are gentle, affectionate creatures that strive to please their masters.

As is to be expected, each breed of pony has its own characteristics. Besides the conformation and personality traits peculiar to specific breeds (which are discussed in Chapter 4), all ponies have a number of common physical features. Whether grade or registered, large or small, streamlined or chunky, used for riding or driving, a pony ideally should be well proportioned with strong, muscular hindquarters and shoulders, have a neck whose length is in proportion to the size of the head, and an alert expression. For a thorough coverage of the anatomy of a horse or pony see *Wonders of the World of Horses*, by Sigmund A. Lavine and Brigid Casey, Dodd, Mead & Company, 1972. Because of space limitations, it will not be repeated in this book.

Varying environments have played an important role in producing pony breeds with differing characteristics. For example, ponies native to cold regions grow thick winter coats, while ponies whose habitat is strewn with boulders develop the ability to jump. Man has had a great influence on the temperament

Note the heavy winter coats on these Connemara ponies photographed on the road at Maam Cross, County Galway. The lead pony has the traditional black points of its ancestors.

and physical appearance of the modern pony. By crossing breeds to produce ponies for specific purposes, he has fixed both desirable and undesirable characteristics. Man is also responsible for making ponies more colorful. Once all ponies were either a dull grayish-brown or yellowish tan, but selective breeding has given to present-day ponies coats of many different hues. Among these are the spotted coat of the Appaloosa and the gleaming golden hide of the Palomino, as well as less spectacular coats of bay, black, brown, buckskin, chestnut, dun, gray, parti-colored, roan, sorrel, and white.

'Tis said, "A good horse is never a bad color." However, it is not always easy to determine a pony's color. For example, completely black ponies (except for white head and leg markings) are rather rare. This is because the presence of any fine brown hairs on the muzzle of a pony that appears to be black automatically classifies the animal as brown.

While certain ponies are evenly colored all over, others have

If a pony has any brown hairs at all, it cannot be classified as black.

"points" of a different shade. To a horseman, "points" are the mane, tail, and lower leg. Generally speaking, the contrasting colors of the coat and the points greatly enhance a pony's appearance.

Colors

Appaloosa   Several breeds of ponies have appaloosa markings—the parti-colored coats typical of the famous horses raised by the Nez Percé Indians. Six basic appaloosa color patterns are recognized (frost, marble, snowflake, leopard, blanket, and spotted blanket), as well as mixtures of two or more patterns. Manes and tails are usually the same hue as the predominate color of the coat. The legs are often spotted. *No two ponies have identical appaloosa markings.*

Bay Bays come in many shades of brown but always have black manes, tails, and points. Those with yellowish-tan coats are called light bays; reddish individuals are known as blood bays. Dark bays—deep brown with tinges of light brown on the inside of the legs—can only be distinguished from brown ponies by their muzzles. Dark bays have reddish muzzles while those of brown ponies are either light brown or dun.

Black As indicated, to be called black a pony must be black all over except for white head or leg markings.

Brown The coats of brown ponies range from a bay-like shade to almost black. Brown ponies generally have black points.

Buckskin Cowboys were the first to call ponies with yellow or gold coats and black points "buckskins." Modern breeders produce buckskins by mating yellowish-tan and bright mahogany bays and hope the foals will have no white markings except on the face and below the knee. They also hope that each foal will have a black stripe down the back and zebra-like striping on the legs.

Chestnut There are many shades of chestnut—pale red-

This chestnut pony has a lighter colored mane and tail.

brown, various shades of gold, a rich deep brown. The lightest chestnut is a golden, the darkest a liver, between these extremes the bright red. Many chestnuts have white markings on the face or lower legs. While manes and tails are usually the same color as the body or slightly lighter, some have silver-blond or white manes and tails.

Dun   As indicated, many prehistoric horses had yellowish-tan coats. Some ponies not only have the body color of their ancestors but also the black points and dorsal stripe of early equines. Other ponies have inherited the black points and the stripe down the back but their coats are not the traditional dun. For example, a mouse dun's coat is lilac-gray, a darker blue dun looks "a washed-out black," while a golden dun is the color of sand.

Gray   Most gray ponies are born brown, sorrel, or almost black. When mature, their coats range from nearly white to a dark steel gray. A close examination re-

An eighteen-year-old gray Shetland stallion. Note the mottling on the body and the light mane and tail.

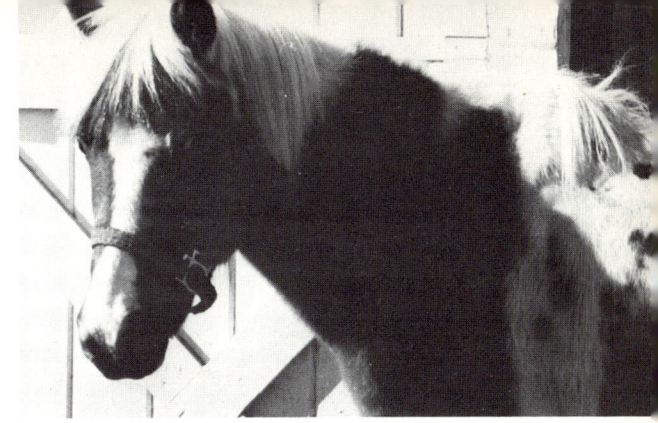

A parti-colored pony

veals that, although gray ponies lighten with age, their coats consist of intermingled black and white hairs. A "flea-bitten" gray's darker hairs are clustered together in small spots all over the body, while an iron gray's black hairs predominate. A light gray's white hairs are more pronounced than its black hairs, while a dapple gray's coat is covered with spots that give a mottled effect. Manes and tails of gray ponies are either black or white, being composed of varying proportions of black and white hairs. Usually, the legs are the color of the body, but can be a dark gray or black.

Palomino   A Palomino is the hue of newly minted gold, and its coat seems to glitter in the sun. The mane and tail are always white. Note: A pony with palomino coloring may turn lighter or darker with age.

Parti-colored   The popular names for ponies whose coats have patches of two or more colors on the white ground color are calico, paint, pinto, and spotted. Technically, ponies whose hides are white overlaid with rather large, irregularly shaped black patches are piebalds. Their legs and tail are black or white, while the mane is black, white, or "patched." If a pony's white coat is covered by big uneven areas of bay, brown, or chestnut, it is a skewbald. The tail is solid colored, the mane white or patched, the legs colored or white.

True white ponies are rare. Most are gray turning white with age. Right, Lucky Strike, a strawberry roan mare standing 13.3, has a mixture of red, yellow, and white hairs.

Roan	A roan's coat is made up of a mixture of colored and white hairs. The differing ratios of these hairs determines what type of roan a pony is. Individuals with red, yellow, and white hairs are known as strawberry roans; those with black, yellow, and white hairs as blue roans; while chestnut, yellow, and white hairs produce the bay brown. Mane and tail are commonly black but can be a mixture of silver and black. Legs are black.

Sorrel	The sorrel and roan are quite similar. However, sorrels lack white hairs, having only red and black ones. Sorrels may be bright yellow, gold, or red. Golden sorrels can be distinguished from Palominos by their manes and tails. As indicated, those of the former are always white while sorrels' manes and tails are the same color as their bodies.

White　　White is not really a color but shows the lack of shading due to the absence of pigment—coloring material found in the cells and tissue of living things. Although many gray ponies turn white or nearly white with age, they are not true white ponies. Such animals are quite rare. Known as albinos, they have no pigment in the skin, hair, or iris of the eye.

When ponies are registered or advertised for sale, the colors of their bodies and points are mentioned. So are certain face markings. Among these are: *star*, a white mark on the forehead; *stripe*, a narrow mark running down the face as far as the nose bones; *blaze*, a broad white mark extending below the nose; and *white faced*, meaning markings on the forehead, muzzle, and cheeks.

Leg markings—which are usually white—are also identified in advertisements and registration papers. A white leg marking that goes up to the knee is called a stocking. A sock only extends to the fetlock (the tufted, cushion-like projection on the back side of the leg above the hoof).

Equine coloration and markings are mentioned in many superstitions. For example, dun-colored ponies are supposedly hard and willing workers, while chestnuts are held to be difficult to control. Meanwhile, horsemen have long recited:

> *Four white legs, keep him not a day,*
> *Three white legs, send him far away.*
> *Two white legs, give him to your friend, but*
> *One white leg—keep him to the end!*

3 History of the Pony

Fossil remains of the horse are common in rocks formed during many different geological periods. Because of this we know more about the evolution of the horse than of any other animal.

Palaeontologists—specialists in the study of fossils—have determined that, of all the animals, the horse is most closely related to the tapir of South America and the rhinoceros of Asia and Africa. Scientists have also established that not only did the horse originate in North America but also that the greater part of its evolution took place in the New World. Further research has revealed that early horses often crossed the land bridge (now flooded by the Bering Straits) that once connected North America to Asia, and that they wandered westward to Europe.

The earliest known horse appeared some sixty million years ago. It was the size of a small dog, lived in forests, and had teeth adapted for browsing on bushes. Popularly called the Dawn Horse, this animal—the ancestor of all present-day ponies and horses—had four toes on the forefeet and three toes on the hindfeet.

As the eons passed, some descendants of the Dawn Horse grew larger. Their legs lengthened but, by extending their long

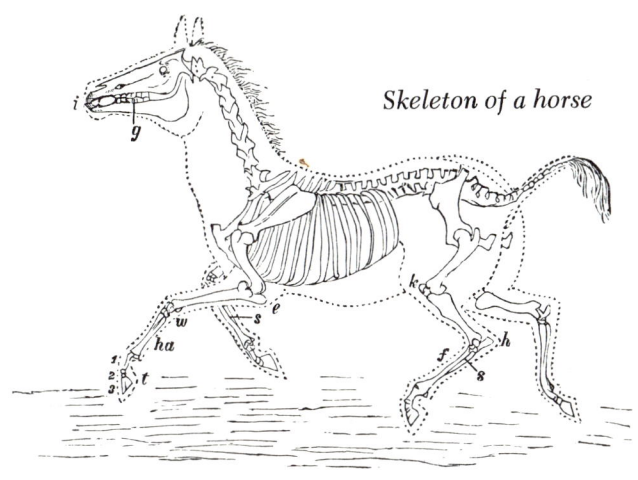

Skeleton of a horse

i, Incisor teeth. *g*, Grinding teeth, with the gap between the two as in all grass-feeders. *k*, Knee. *h*, Hock or heel. *f*, Foot. *s*, Splints or remains of the two lost toes. *e*, Elbow. *w*, Wrist. *h*, Hand-bone. *t*, middle toe of three joints, 1, 2, 3 forming the hoof.

necks, they were able to reach low-growing grasses, which they shredded with teeth modified for grinding. Among the changes in the structure of the body was a reduction in the number of toes. Eventually there was only one toe on each foot which was enclosed in a hoof. Meanwhile, the complexity of the brain increased.

But not all branches of the horse's family tree prospered. Many of the animals, unable to adjust to changing climatic conditions, died. Still, the evolution of the survivors continued. When the Pleistocene period began a million years ago, several species of horses existed. However, the only horse remaining at the end of the Pleistocene epoch was *Pliohippus*, which closely resembled the modern pony in structure, size, and shape.

Pliohippus was the progenitor of the first true horse, known to science as *Equus*. Palaeontologists estimate that the evolution of the Dawn Horse into the hard-hoofed *Equus* of the present day took approximately fifty million years.

Unlike many of the early horses that had migrated to Eurasia across the land bridge, *Equus* flourished in the Old World. This was indeed fortunate, as otherwise there would be no horses in the world today. Although North America was the center of the evolution of the horse, all horses vanished from the New World less than a million years ago. No one knows the reason why.

Meanwhile, *Equus* roamed far and wide. Fossils reveal the extent of its wanderings throughout Africa, Asia, and Europe. So do the piles of bones dug up at campsites occupied by Stone Age men who hunted horses for meat. Ancient man also pictured horses on cliffs and on walls of caves. These drawings, along with the fossils and bones, provide evidence that *Equus* split into three groups with differing physical characteristics. The first group was composed of thick-coated, heavy-boned, slow-moving animals that grazed on the flat lands of northwest Europe. According to some authorities, these horses were the immediate ancestors of huge draft horses such as the Clydesdales and Percherons.

Other experts, however, maintain that draft horses are descendants of a race of *Equus* that lived in Asia—thick-legged horses that survived until modern times. They are called Przewalsky's horse after the Russian explorer who discovered

Old print shows Przewalsky's horse, forerunner of heavy draft horses.

Tarpan herd in Germany, where zoologists scientifically recreated this extinct ancestor of modern ponies

them on the edge of the Gobi Desert in Mongolia in 1881. In all probability no purebred Przewalsky's horse exists in the wild state at the present time. However, a considerable number of purebreds are displayed in zoos throughout the world. Their appearance and coloration are exactly the same as those of horses drawn by prehistoric man in Pleistocene times—small, stocky, deep chested, with coarse heads, slightly tufted tails, and crestlike manes. The body is a reddish tan which fades to a creamy white on the belly. Zebra-like markings may show on the legs, while a more or less distinct black stripe runs down the back. Horsemen call this dorsal marking an "eel stripe."

The eel stripe is the outstanding physical characteristic of the Tarpan. This horse once grazed on the steppes of northern Europe and southern Russia. Unlike Przewalsky's horse, the

Tarpan—forebear of light, fine-legged breeds of horses—is a handsome animal. The body is mousy gray; the legs, nose, and tail are black. Often both the inner thighs and legs are barred and the entire coat becomes almost white in winter.

Were it not for German zoologists, the Tarpan would be extinct. The last wild specimen was shot late in the nineteenth century, and no Tarpan was displayed in any zoo at that time. After studying drawings, reading old descriptions, and examining countless Tarpan bones and skulls, the zoologists launched a most unusual project. First, a herd of horses with distinctive Tarpan characteristics was rounded up. Then a complicated program of crossbreeding these animals was begun under controlled conditions with the aim of scientifically recreating the original Tarpan. The task took thirty years. Proof that present-day Tarpans do not differ from the extinct wild stock is furnished not only by the animals' conformation and coloration but also by X-ray photographs. The latter reveal that the skull, bones, and teeth of the "new Tarpan" are identical with those of mounted specimens of wild Tarpans displayed in various museums.

Authorities agree that modern ponies are kin to the Tarpan, the degree of relationship varying from breed to breed. But the immediate ancestor of present-day ponies was a short-legged, broad-headed, small-eared, bushy-tailed pony native to northern Europe. While this chunky, powerful animal had some of the characteristics of Przewalsky's horse, it owed most of its features to the Tarpan. Known as the Celtic pony, it inhabited the Hebrides, Ireland, and Scotland, as well as parts of the European mainland.

With the possible exception of the Shetland pony—which may be the only prehistoric species of pony still living—there is little doubt that crossbreeding Celtic ponies with horses from the Orient and Mongolia produced ponies not only native to the

The Shetland may be the only prehistoric species of pony in existence.

British Isles but also to lands as far apart as Iceland and Greece.

The stocky Celtic pony amazed Julius Caesar when he invaded England in 55 B.C. Not only was the great conqueror impressed with the pony's stamina when used as a pack animal but also he marveled at its speed and courage when drawing chariots on the battlefield. However, after many centuries passed, British ponies had no value in time of war except to carry material. The cumbersome armor worn by medieval warriors was too heavy for their small bodies to bear. To increase the ponies' size and strength, they were bred with horses imported from Europe—but that attempt failed.

Thus, when Henry the Eighth was crowned King of England in A.D. 1509, he ordered his foresters to inspect Britain's herds of semi-wild ponies and destroy any mares too small to bear foals of "a reasonable stature." Fortunately the foresters found combing moors, mountains, commons, heaths, and woods for grazing ponies a most difficult task. Nor could they rely on the assistance of the independent farmers, who cared little whether or not His Majesty had enough "Great Horses." The combination of public apathy and the lack of enthusiasm with which the foresters performed their duty had two results: The number of horses suitable for cavalry use was not increased, and the future of native British ponies was assured. The saving of these animals was vital to the history of the pony—generally speaking, they became the foundation stock of most modern pony breeds.

4 Pony Breeds

Almost every country can boast of a native pony bred to perform specific tasks under certain environmental and climatic conditions. Many of these ponies have felt the tug of reins for hundreds of years, while some have only recently entered the service of man.

The origins, physical characteristics, temperaments, and even the names of a number of breeds of ponies are practically unknown outside their native lands. It is doubtful that many people have heard of the Batak pony of Indonesia, the Pindos pony of Greece, or the Kathiawari and Manipur ponies of India.

No book of this size is large enough to tell the history of all the breeds, describe them, and detail their uses. Therefore the ponies corralled in this chapter have been limited to the most popular breeds in the United States and the British Isles. The descriptions given are based on American standards for each breed. However, differences between American and English standards have been noted.

SHETLAND

The Shetland, often referred to as the Sheltie, is the most popular breed of pony. Its small size, patience, rugged constitution, gentleness, and lovable disposition make the sturdy

A beautiful chestnut Shetland driving pony

Shetland the ideal mount for small children. Nor is the Sheltie overlooked by adults, who use the diminutive animal as a pack pony, a circus performer, or as a willing competitor on weight-pulling contests, trotting races, and the show ring.

Although the Shetland bears the name of a group of barren, windswept islands off Scotland's north coast, some of its ancestors were imported by Scandinavians who had established settlements along those storm-tossed coastlines at a very early date. Other progenitors of the Shetland were the horses the Romans left behind when they withdrew from the British Isles in A.D. 410. But in all probability the Norsemen who then occupied parts of Iceland, Scotland, the Hebrides, and the Orkneys supplied the original stock—small Celtic-type ponies.

No breed of pony developed under more adverse conditions. Because grazing was poor, Shetlands learned to eat seaweed tossed onto the shore by waves. During the severe winter months—the Arctic Circle is only 350 miles away—the tough ponies pawed through the snow to find a scant mouthful of grass and grew long shaggy coats that protected them from the bitter cold. Shelties also developed a "shawl"—a growth of strong hairs at the base of the tail. When a pony stands with its tail to the wind in foul weather, the shawl spreads out protectively over the hind legs.

Because English fanciers want their Shetlands to look like miniature draft horses, the traditional Sheltie bred in the British Isles has a blocky conformation due to the broad back, thick neck and shoulders, relatively short barrel (the body between the fore and hind legs), and the heavy-boned legs. On the other hand, American horsemen breed finer Shetlands for the show ring and for use as children's mounts. Because these animals have slimmer barrels than their British kin, they are easier for youngsters to ride.

Shetlands come in all colors. The breed is famous for its chestnut, golden, and silver dapples. Dappled Shetlands always have white tails and manes.

One of the authors meets her first equine, a young part Shetland.

Connemara

Rock-strewn fields, craggy hills, and peat bogs are commonplace in Connemara in County Galway on the west coast of Ireland. Bands of ponies have roamed over this rugged landscape for centuries. In search of forage, they leap from ledge to ledge and deftly avoid being mired in wet, spongy ground. During the winter months when violent westerly winds sweep in from the cold Atlantic Ocean, Connemara ponies seek shelter in damp caves, narrow "doreens" (little roads), or huddle together behind huge rocks or thatched cottages that break the force of the wind.

This constant battle to survive resulted in the development of a strong, sturdy breed with a hearty constitution and keen instincts. Moreover, because of being constantly forced to cross slippery outcrops and leap over boulders or "cashels" (mounds of rock) while grazing, the Connemara—sometimes called the

Connemara pony mare and foal graze among the rocks.

Hobbie—has become surefooted and an outstanding jumper. These characteristics make the breed an ideal mount for cross-country riding, point-to-point racing, and show jumping.

Like many an Irish tale, the history of the Connemara is a blend of fact and tradition. Some authorities believe that the original stock consisted of hardy ponies brought to Ireland's west coast by Scandinavian settlers. Others say Connemaras derived from Mongolian stock and were probably the oldest equine inhabitants of the British Isles. Still others maintain they are of Icelandic origin. According to the experts, these early ponies of whatever origin were eventually crossed with Spanish horses shipped to the port of Galway, which was the center of a thriving trade with Spain during the sixteenth and seventeenth centuries.

Legend does not agree with the experts. It maintains that the Spanish horses that mated with the ponies of Connemara never saw Galway city. According to legend, the free-roaming Connemara ponies mated with the horses that swam ashore when the Spanish Armada was sunk off the Irish coast in A.D. 1588.

Despite the conflict of legend and expert, one thing is certain—the modern Connemara has Spanish blood. It also owes much to the Arabians to which the ponies were frequently bred until the middle of the nineteenth century. Similarly, the introduction of Welsh cob blood enhanced the Connemara's conformation.

However, years of outcrossing with other breeds eventually brought the Connemara to the brink of extinction. In the 1920's, therefore, a group of fanciers decided to refine the Connemara by selective breeding and formed the Connemara Pony Breeders Association. Approved stallions were mated to approved mares and their get was turned loose to graze in the traditional way of Connemara ponies. For two and a half years these animals received no attention from their owners. Then the survivors were rounded up and the best of them became the foundation stock for the modern Connemara.

The Connemara is almost impossible to keep fenced because it jumps for the sheer love of jumping. Standing only 11 to 14.2 hands, the breed has consistently outjumped much bigger horses at international shows. This is because the Connemara has powerful hindquarters that hurl it into the air, as well as large sloping shoulders that provide the initial spring and absorb the shock of the landing. The breed also has tremendous courage.

At one time Connemara ponies were dun in color and had a

Although too tall to be classified as a pony, Dublin, an international level dressage horse, was sired by a full-blooded Connemara pony stallion.

The pony in this painting by Richard Dupont won many prizes in 12.2 classes in England. Nuts and May was bred in County Tipperary, Ireland, and was classified a skewbald. He had a very kind temperament.

black dorsal stripe. The mane and tail were also black. Many still have this coloration. Others are bay, cream, gray, or black or brown with white markings. A small number have roan or chestnut coats. Piebalds and skewbalds are not unknown.

Welsh

The Welsh pony has two claims to fame. Not only is it recognized as "just about the most versatile of all modern ponies and horses" but also it has the oldest *recorded* history of any breed of pony native to the British Isles. Over two thousand years ago the inhabitants of Wales were using this gentle, hardy, strong, and extremely intelligent animal to carry loads in peace and to haul chariots in time of war.

When Caesar invaded England in 55 B.C. he was so impressed with the ponies of his Welsh foes that he sent several back to Rome. Caesar also personally trained some to pull chariots and established a farm in western Wales where native ponies were crossed with Oriental and Arabian horses in hopes of producing a pack pony for his legions. Meanwhile, the Welsh, who had retreated into the mountains, were allowing bands of their ponies to graze in a semi-wild state. Because the ponies competed with sheep for grass, farmers killed many of them. But the bands still ranged far and wide (foals were rounded up each fall) and the ponies developed tremendous powers of endurance, hardiness, resistance to disease, and became famous for their surefootedness. The latter characteristic plus their habitat led to the breed's becoming known as Welsh Mountain ponies.

Eventually, inbreeding led to a decline in the quality of the free-running bands. To improve it, Arabian, Hackney, and Thoroughbred stallions were bred to Welsh Mountain mares during the eighteenth and nineteenth centuries. This had the desired effect, but it changed the ponies' appearance. Arabian blood gave them slightly dished faces, very soft muzzles, long

Ponies graze in the mountains of Wales.

A handsome Welsh pony

arched necks, small pointed ears, and high-set proudly carried tails.

Originally, the Welsh Mountain pony stood twelve hands or under but the introduction of Hackney and Thoroughbred blood made it taller. As a result, it was decided to divide registered ponies into various groups—called sections—based on their height.

There are now four types of Welsh ponies and they all are a delight to the eye. This is particularly true when they trot in harness. In this gait (Welsh walk and canter like other breeds) they do not pull their legs upward but throw them straight forward from the shoulders. As they do so, their hooves are so low that they barely skim over the ground. Horsemen call this gliding action "daisy cutting."

Exmoor and Dartmoor

Native to the British Isles, Exmoor and Dartmoor ponies make excellent hunting and children's ponies. Both are sturdy, hardy animals that have tremendous stamina.

The Exmoor is a direct descendant of the ponies that roamed the islands after crossing the land bridge that once connected England to the continent of Europe. It was first domesticated by the ancient Celts who used it as a pack pony and to draw their chariots.

Exmoor is a high moorland in southwestern England whose boundaries enclose an ancient forest and large tracts of uncultivated land. Here huntsmen mounted on Exmoor ponies chase the famous Exmoor stags across the picturesque countryside. Swift, strong, and sturdy—although stunted because of its habitat—the small Exmoor (mares stand 12.2 hands; stallions, 12.3 hands) easily keeps up with large horses specifically bred for hunting.

Exmoor pony stallion in summer

Supreme champion Dartmoor pony stallion. Overseas visitors are most welcome at the summer Dartmoor Pony Society shows in England.

No Exmoor pony should have white markings. Its coat—which becomes wiry in winter—should be bay, brown, or mouse dun in color with black points. Characteristic of the breed is the pale oaten shading around the eye and on the muzzle, belly, and inside of the thigh. This coloration, technically called "mealy," is inherited from the wild horses that once roamed Mongolia.

Like the Exmoor, the Dartmoor pony is a native of the high moors of southwestern England. An ancient resident of a region constantly swept by winds bearing cold, mist, and rain, the Dartmoor has had to be extremely hardy in order to survive. It is a sound, tough pony whose shaggy thick coat sheds water as efficiently as a new-laid roof. Because the Dartmoor has a short, strong back, powerful shoulders, muscular hindquarters, and stout legs, it can carry very heavy loads. In fact, the breed was used for a pack pony long before it was harnessed or ridden.

The Dartmoor's muscular physique catches the eye. Meanwhile, the small, well-set head, alert ears, full mane, bushy forelock, and high-set tail give it an attractive appearance. Some of the breed's characteristics are the result of crossbreeding.

However, crossbreeding the Dartmoor with other ponies and with Arabian and Thoroughbred horses debased the breed. As a result, it began to lose its traditional strength and vigor. Therefore most breeders of Dartmoors have stopped the practice in hopes their stock will regain the tough qualities of their ancestors.

Dartmoors may be any color except piebald or skewbald. The preferred colors are bay, black, and brown. Gray Dartmoors are not unusual, but chestnut or dun specimens are rare. Like all native British ponies, the Dartmoor is a small, unusually strong animal. The average pony stands between 11.2 and 12 hands—no pony taller that 12.2 hands can be registered.

NEW FOREST

One of Great Britain's most beautiful national parks is the New Forest in southern England. Much of this preserve consists of woodlands, bog, and heath over which approximately three thousand ponies roam.

Ancient laws provide that owners have the right to let their animals run freely through the New Forest providing they are kept within certain boundaries. Ponies that are not are seized and a fine is levied. Modern engineering helps contain the ponies. Wherever a road leaves the New Forest, a hoof-hurting grating blocks the way. Actually, few ponies have to be impounded. Each band of New Forest ponies has its own territory and usually stays within its limits. All New Forest ponies are branded or marked in some way by their owners. This makes it easy to identify stock during the annual pony drifts (roundups) that take place each fall. At this time foals are branded and

A band of New Forest ponies

excess animals sold to those seeking general-purpose ponies.

New Forest ponies are mentioned in manuscripts written during the reign of Canute (A.D. 1016-1035). But the breed had been established long before Canute ruled England. It probably was developed from the ancient native pony of Britain. The oriental-type head and other physical features of the sure-footed New Forest pony can be traced back to infusions of Arabian and Thoroughbred blood.

The New Forest pony stands between 12 and 14 hands tall. While all colors except piebald and skewbald are found, browns and bays are the most common. Many specimens have an eel stripe.

DALES AND FELL

Extending southward from the Scottish border, the Pennine Chain (an extensive range of hills) roughly splits northern England in half. The hills also separate the habitats of two closely related breeds of ponies—the Dales and the Fell. The Dales pony ranges on the east side of the Pennines, the Fell on the west.

Both breeds probably had the same ancestors—the heavy

A Fell pony by famed horse artist Sam Savitt

Frisian horses the Romans introduced into England and bred to native ponies. While the Fell is usually smaller than the Dales pony, both are exceptionally strong and powerful animals.

The Dales pony has a short neck, straight shoulders, strong muscular back, and well-sprung ribs. The tail is not set as high as those of other moorland breeds, while the fetlocks are covered with long, fine hairs called feathers. Bay, brown, and jet black in color (occasionally with white markings), the Dale is one of the most attractive of ponies.

Because of its great strength, the Dales pony is often ridden by adults, yet is so gentle it makes an excellent mount for children.

The Fell pony, too, has an eye-catching conformation. In addition to feathers, the breed has a full mane and carries the low-set tail gaily. While most Fell ponies are black, brown specimens are seen from time to time, but bay Fell ponies with mealy noses are quite rare.

Although the Fell pony was once used solely as a pack animal, its action is quite comfortable. As a result, it is a popular riding pony.

Pony of the Americas

This pony was "manufactured" to meet a specific need—a western-type stock pony for older teens. The breeders who created the Pony of the Americas set out to produce a stylish, colorful, and useful pony. They achieved their aim by extensive crossbreeding. The POA, as this pony is popularly called, owes its size to the Shetland, its conformation to the Arabian and Quarter Horse, and its brilliant coloring to the Appaloosa. While all six basic Appaloosa markings are found in the POA, the spotted blanket (dark spots sprinkled over a white area) is most common. No POA can be registered if it has pinto or albino coloration.

In addition to its distinctive coloring, the breed has other characteristics that make it easy to recognize. The POA has

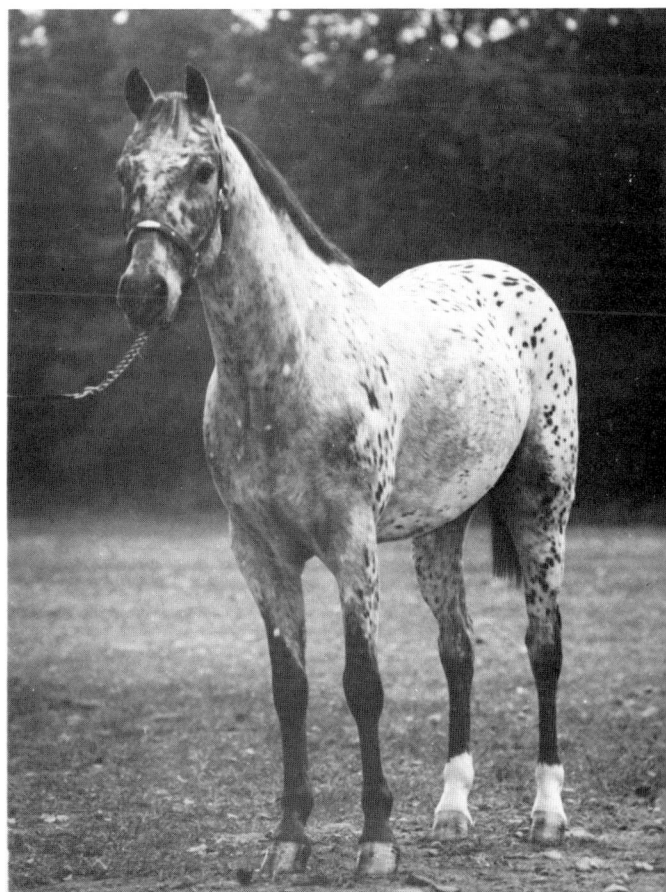

Pony of the Americas gelding

mottled or spotted skin around the lips and nostrils, narrow black and white stripes on at least one hoof, a rather sparse tail and mane, a white eyeball around a colored iris, and varnish marks. The latter, which resemble wet stains, are actually dark hairs. Varnish marks (also known as marbling) appear above the eyes and on the face, nose, hips, and the outsides of the hind legs.

The POA's slightly dished face, refined head, large prominent eyes, and alert pointed ears stem from its Arabian blood. So does its conformation, which ideally should blend the lines of the Arabian and the Quarter House. The two-inch difference between the maximum height of a POA and the minimum height of a registered Appaloosa (fifty-six inches) is a deliberate attempt to distinguish between the two breeds.

Because the POA is fundamentally a stock horse it is ridden Western style and its mane is roached (trimmed to form an arc of upright bristles), as is the mane of a Quarter Horse. A patch of long hair is allowed to grow over the withers for use as a handhold when mounting and dismounting.

An outstanding utility pony, the POA is used for trail riding, racing—they are only two seconds slower than a Quarter Horse—and jumping. But the majority of POA's are exhibited. Young riders monopolize the performance classes. Among the latter are several events in which riders dress in Indian or cowboy costumes. But it is the skill and stamina of the ponies that are judged as the POA's engage in activities such as barrel racing and calf cutting.

No performance class is more popular than the Trail Class in which pony and rider simulate a trail ride. While the rider has to open and close gates without dismounting, the pony has even harder tasks. It has to avoid obstacles, jump or sidestep potholes, back through narrow gaps, and perform other tasks that not only reveal its training but also its temperament.

FALABELLA

Because the Falabella family failed to keep records of its early attempts to create a miniature breed of ponies on their ranch in Argentina, the ancestry of this pony is uncertain. However, it is known that the foundation stock was Shetland and, in all probability, it was bred to native ponies. There is no doubt that a number of breeds contributed to the development of the Falabella. For example, Appaloosa markings are quite common.

The majority of midget ponies are the result of inbreeding extremely small Shetlands. The foals produced by this mating of close relatives of the same family are generally misshapen and may have an internal deformity. Therefore most horsemen are convinced that midget ponies are without "any redeeming feature but smallness."

Falabellas resemble tiny toy horses.

On the other hand, the Falabella, which is only thirty inches (7.2 hands) or less tall, is a beautiful, well-proportioned animal. The result of more than a century of linebreeding and outcrossing, the 120-pound Falabella, unlike most other midget ponies, will not become bigger if fed all it can eat.

Falabellas breed true. No baby animal is more charming than their foals. Weighing about a pound and standing approximately eight inches high, they resemble tiny toy horses and, like toys, they can be held in one hand. Foals as well as their parents make gentle and affectionate pets.

Although the Falabella can be ridden by small children or employed to pull specially designed carts, it is widely used as a performer by its owners. An extremely intelligent and expensive pony, it can be taught a long list of tricks in a very short time. The Falabella also excels as a jumper, being able to leap as high as its head.

HAFLINGER

This native of the Austrian Alps has been described as "a prince in front and a peasant behind." There is good reason. The Haflinger has a most attractive head (due to its Arabian ancestors), with large lively eyes, small ears, and a full flaxen or white mane that contrasts with its golden chestnut coat. But the Haflinger has the body of a pack pony—strong quarters and broad back supported by short, sturdy legs.

A typical surefooted mountain pony standing between 13.2 and 14 hands high, the Haflinger is a compact, rugged animal possessing tremendous strength. For centuries it has been engaged in general farm work at altitudes of five to seven thousand feet and employed by lumbermen to snake logs out of the woods or to haul loads.

In addition to serving man in time of peace, this willing, versatile, and easy-going pony has long been enlisted to move

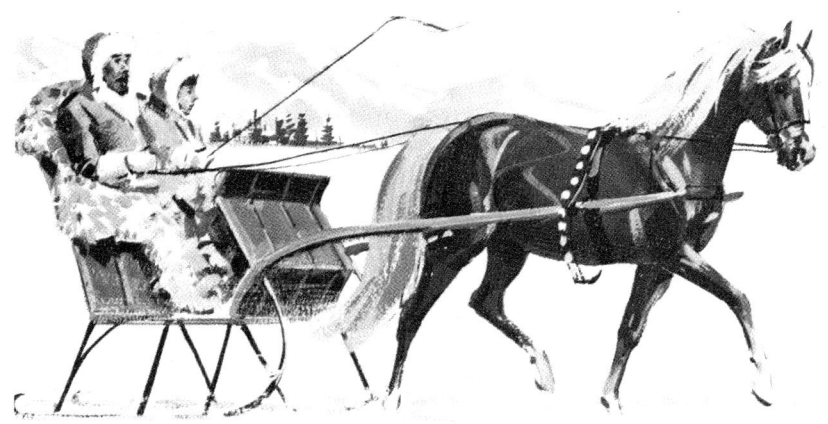
A Haflinger pony, by Sam Savitt

military stores. Not only is the Haflinger capable of packing or hauling ammunition and other supplies fifty or sixty miles a day in good weather but also it can perform well when roads are blocked with snow and the temperature below zero. No wonder the Austrian Army calls its four-wheel-drive vehicles Haflingers!

Along with being in great demand whenever a rugged pack or draft pony can be used, the Haflinger is widely employed for riding. Its long, ground-eating stride gives a smooth and exceptionally comfortable ride. This is most unusual for a pony—most of them have short, choppy gaits. Further, this breed is ideal as a circus performer.

Chincoteague

Ponies long have roamed over Assateague Island off the north Virginia coast. No one knows for sure how and when they reached lonely Assateague, but legend provides two explanations. One says Indian ponies found their way to the island at a very early date. The second holds that the Spanish government shipped some Moorish horses from Africa to Peru in the sixteenth century to work in the gold mines. The galleon carrying the horses sank in a storm off the Virginia coast. Although no humans escaped from the wreck, some of the horses managed to swim to Assateague.

Legend may explain how ponies reached Assateague but it does not tell why they are called Chincoteague ponies. The reason is that the residents of Chincoteague Island (which is separated from uninhabited Assateague by a narrow channel) have been rounding up the ponies and selling them since the early 1700's.

Today, the so-called Pony Pennings attract thousands of tourists. Pony Penning Day is held annually on the last Thursday of July under the auspices of the Chincoteague Volunteer Fire Department. In preparation for the event, volunteer "cowboys" ride through the fields and woodlands of Assateague and herd the ponies toward the south end of the island where they are hazed into corrals, fed, watered, and kept overnight.

At low tide the following morning the ponies are forced into the water and made to swim between two lines of boats across the channel to Chincoteague, a quarter of a mile away. Foals less than eight weeks old make the trip by boat. The animals are driven down the main street of Chincoteague and placed in corrals. An auction is then held, with the proceeds going to the fire department. The next day unsold ponies and stock reserved for breeding are herded back to Assateague.

According to early records, the ponies of Assateague stood about 14 hands and were drab in color. However, letting Shetlands run with them decreased their size. Outcrossing with Shetlands also produced the odd pinto patterns that presently predominate, although bay, black, gray, and sorrel specimens are common.

An infusion of Welsh blood led to the ponies' becoming smaller and, in addition, gave them dapple-gray coats. The Welsh

Chincoteague ponies photographed on Assateague

ponies turned loose on Assateague also improved the heads and necks of the native stock. Nevertheless, Chincoteague ponies lack a standard conformation. Chunky animals, they have many of the characteristics of stunted horses—which gives some credence to the romantic account of the wrecked galleon.

The chances are excellent that the Chincoteague pony is destined to lose its potty body and become taller and more streamlined. Since 1966 when the famous gray Arabian stallion Skowreym was bred to Assateague's outstanding mares, efforts have been made to improve the substance and style of America's best-loved ponies.

Hackney

In this era of sports cars there is little demand for a high-stepping trotter capable of drawing carriages at a fast gait through city streets. As a result, the Hackney horse has practically vanished. But the popularity of the Hackney pony—the product of linebreeding small Hackney horses—increases each year. Yet the Hackney pony is rarely ridden, is almost never raced, is infrequently harnessed to a cart, and is hardly ever jumped.

Nevertheless, the Hackney pony has no rival for the title bestowed upon it by horsemen—the Prince of Ponies. The breed has "personality plus" and, as a result, reigns supreme as the most elegant, graceful, and stylish of show harness ponies.

But the Hackney is no pony for younger horse lovers. Not only is the breed extremely high strung but also its training requires a great deal of time as well as considerable knowledge. Then, too, it takes expert skill to drive Hackneys properly—particularly when they are hitched in pairs or tandem so that they can display their spirited trot to best advantage.

Actually, the action of the Hackney is exaggerated. When well trained, properly shod, correctly harnessed, and dexterously driven, a Hackney pony raises its legs vigorously, smoothly flings them forward (the hind hoof almost hitting the belly, the front knee nearly level with the chin), hesitates for a second or two, then snaps the legs downward into position for the next stride.

The Hackney is a large pony, usually standing between 13 and 14 hands. While black or brown individuals are not uncommon, bay is the characteristic color of the breed. Most Hackneys have white markings on the legs and head. Because they have bright, bold, and prominent eyes, small ears that point well forward, and rather well-chisled heads (although Roman-nosed), Hackney ponies give the impression of being extremely alert.

Icelandic

When adventurous pioneers of Norwegian extraction colonized Iceland at the end of the ninth century after Christ, they imported ponies. These animals were of Celtic stock and it is entirely probable they were identical to the ponies used by the

A pair of Hackneys

Norsemen who had founded settlements in northern Ireland, Scotland, and the Hebrides and Orkney Islands.

Until comparatively recent times the ponies of Iceland were isolated from other equines. As a result, the half-wild herds of ponies that range over that island's rugged lowlands and lava-strewn hillsides closely resemble their ancient ancestors. Actually, it is remarkable that free-ranging ponies have been able to live in Iceland for centuries. Not only did they have to withstand the rigors of extremely harsh winters but also they had to be content with a diet of coarse grass and twigs enriched by fish cast up on the shore during storms. Although muscular and strong, thousands of Icelandic ponies have perished during exceptionally cold winters. Because only specimens with tre-

Icelandic pony and owner

mendous stamina and vitality have been able to endure the bite of frigid winds and the lack of food, it is little wonder that the surviving stock is very sturdy, highly intelligent, and independent in character.

Standing between 11 and 13 hands, with a rather thick neck, large nose, and a stocky body supported by short legs, the Icelandic pony is not an attractive animal. But no pony is more indifferent to fatigue or has more endurance. Nor is any breed of riding pony better gaited. In addition to walking, trotting, and cantering, the Icelandic pony has a characteristic gait called the *tølt*. This ambling trot is not only comfortable for the rider but also it is ground covering.

The *tølt* is the main reason why the Icelandic pony is used for trail riding in the United States and trekking in Iceland and Scandinavia. In the latter lands, a trekking party—often consisting of a group of families—may cover as many as forty miles a day for several weeks as it rides beside glaciers, along lakes flowing past volcanic mountains, and through meadows covered with wildflowers.

5 Pony Lore

Horses have figured in mythology and folklore since ancient times. It is probably safe to assume that the horses mentioned, especially the earlier ones, were actually pony sized.

The ancient peoples of the Far East worshiped horses and often used them for religious sacrifices. Among these were the Hindus, Tibetans, and Mongols. The early Greeks and Romans also held the horse in high esteem and associated it with their gods and goddesses.

In Greek mythology, divinities often assumed the shape of a horse, or a pony. Both Poseidon, god of the sea who created the first horse, and Athene, goddess of wisdom who taught man how to tame it, could become horse-shaped at will. Demeter, personification of Earth's fruitfulness, often was shown with a horse's head. Apollo, the sun god, was drawn from east to west every day by a pair of horses.

Pegasus is perhaps the most famous animal in Greek mythology. It is said this winged horse was born of sea foam. There is a constellation named for Pegasus in the skies of the Northern Hemisphere.

The centaur of Greek mythology was a creature with the

Pegasus, the winged horse

body and legs of a horse and the torso and head of a man. (Ting-lings are the Chinese equivalent.) Hippocampi were horses with the hind parts of a fish. Roman mythology in many instances closely followed the Greek with only the names changed.

Horses played an important part in the mythology of the Norsemen, most of whose mounts were of Icelandic or Norse stock and thus pony sized. Odin, father of the gods, rode Sleipnir, a coal-black pony. Sleipnir was able to travel on both land and sea and was faster than the wind. This may have been due to the fact that Sleipnir had eight legs.

Heimdall, brother of Thor, the war god, rode a silver pony with a golden mane. Gulltopp, or Golden Top, carried his master along the rainbow. Whenever there is a rainbow, Heimdall, the giant killer who will sound his horn at the end of the world, and Gulltopp are probably riding somewhere along it, so it pays to look closely.

The Norse gods decided they needed protection because

they were afraid of the Frost giants. The mischievous god Loki hired a dwarf to build an impenetrable fortress in heaven within a year. The dwarf brought a horse, Svadilfari, with him on the job. Svadilfari would drag mountains up by their roots and the dwarf put them in place in the structure. (Perhaps it is Svadilfari, pulling up mountains, that causes earthquakes.) As the work was nearing completion, the gods decided the payment demanded by the dwarf was too high, and they wanted Loki to cancel the contract. So Loki turned loose a mare that ran into the forest, and Svadilfari disappeared after her. The dwarf couldn't get the job done in time, and when the gods discovered that he was really a giant in disguise they sent him to Niffleheim, which was their version of hell—always dark and cold.

In the Norse heaven dwelled the Valkyries, beautiful warlike maidens who flew down from their mountain home on ponies to gather the souls of slain warriors and guide them to Valhalla, home of Odin. It was believed that the light flashing from their armor as they rode caused the Aurora Borealis, the Northern Lights.

The people of the British Isles, as well as the Gauls and Teutons, long worshiped Eopna, guardian of horses. But as Christianity spread across Europe, the cult of Eopna vanished. However, many still feared mythical horses.

The *aughiska* are the Irish water horses that come galloping out of the waves, most often in November. If you capture one, bridle it, and keep it from the sea, it makes a fine pony. The only drawback is that, if an *aughisky* catches a glimpse of the ocean, back it will go into the waves, taking the rider along and later eating him for dinner!

Across the Irish Sea, a certain Scottish water spirit disguised as a horse is known as a kelpie. Sources differ as to what happens when a kelpie is sighted. One version says that whoever

Not aughiska, *the much feared mythical Irish water horses, but a Connemara mare and her foal*

sees it is doomed to die, while another says that the kelpie, when sighted, becomes docile and a good worker. The *each-uisge* is a Scottish water spirit that gives a ride to doom, disappearing into the sea . . . with only the rider's liver floating back to shore!

The Welsh and the Manx also have tales of water spirits disguised as horses. The nygel, or noggle, of the Shetland Isles are mischievous beasts, so riders should beware. These water horses carry their tails curled up like half wheels, and this should be warning enough to stay away!

English mythology includes the shagfoal and tatterfoal of Lincolnshire, and the colt-pixy of Hampshire and Somerset. The first two are black, fiery-eyed beasts that attack travelers. The colt-pixy is a spirit horse that leads other horses into swamps but also guards orchards and chases apple thieves!

This American pony looks mischievous enough to be a noggle or a colt-pixy from the British Isles.

Horses have been featured in literature since earliest antiquity. The Bible refers to horses that are "swifter than eagles," and Homer mentioned horses in the *Iliad*. It is likely that the horse referred to in the Koran was an Arabian, which would make it pony sized. In one of Plato's dialogues he described women as horses—nice to look at but not very useful! Obviously Plato had not heard of women's rights.

Other poets besides Homer have been inspired by equines, from the ancient past to the present. Virgil, Ovid, Chaucer, Scott, Tennyson, Blake, Cowper, Longfellow, and Stephen Vincent Benét are a few of the more famous ones.

John Steinbeck's *The Red Pony* is a well-known work about a pony, as is "The Maltese Cat" by Rudyard Kipling. Perhaps the most enchanting of all literary ponies was Merrylegs, from Anna Sewell's classic, *Black Beauty*. One of the most famous children's books about a pony is *Misty of Chincoteague*, by

Ponies are popular as an art form.

A magnificent specimen of a Welsh pony from Washington State

Marguerite Henry. This story, later made into a movie, tells of the desire of two children to own Misty, a wild mare from Assateague Island.

Ponies have been featured in many works of art. A Persian miniature, "The Sons of Shal Jehan," shows the youngest of the sons riding on a pony. Famous painters such as Velasquez, Gericault, Morland, Dufy, Renoir, and Stubbs have all painted ponies.

In other forms of media, ponies have been popular. The first pony to gain stardom in the movies was Fritz. He was a Pinto belonging to William S. Hart. Doubles weren't used in Hollywood in those early days, so the pair did such stunts as jumping off cliffs, diving into ice-filled rivers, and riding through plate glass windows. Fritz was so popular that he eventually became the star, not Hart, in the movies the two made together.

One of Walt Disney's TV shows, *Ride a Wild Pony*, featured a Welsh pony and two children, each of whom had a claim to him. And in the world of cartoons, Norman Thelwell is a modern British artist who depicts comic situations between children and ponies to the delight and amusement of all.

6 When Is a Pony Not a Pony?

When is a pony not a pony? When it is a polo pony, an Indian pony, a cow pony, an outrider pony—or when it was in the Pony Express. These are some of the more common misnamed mounts. The thing to remember is that in these cases the term pony is an inherited one, denoting a type rather than a specific breed.

Polo Ponies

Manuscripts show that the game of polo (*pulu*—Tibetan for ball) was played earlier than 600 B.C. Any equine could do as a mount then, but small native ponies were favored. Through the centuries the game became more of an organized sport, and the mounts increased in importance.

Polo reached an all time high in popularity in India during the 1860's. Mongolian stock ponies were used then. Their height was restricted to fifty-four inches because it was felt that "the shorter the mount the easier to reach the ball." By the time polo became widespread in England and the United States, speed, stamina, and a catlike ability to turn and follow the ball were of prime importance in a pony. The size limit was dropped, and mounts became much larger. However, players soon found the larger mounts did not have the hardiness and strength necessary for the game. Pony blood for stamina as well as Thoroughbred for speed and Quarter Horse for maneuverability were all necessary for a good polo mount. Today Griffins, the tough little Mongolian ponies once popular for polo, are again much in demand for polo stock.

INDIAN PONIES

As America was explored and colonized, another type of equine became known as a pony. This was the mount of the Native American Indian. The horse had been reintroduced to America by the Spaniards during their expeditions of the fifteenth and sixteenth centuries. At first the Indians were terrified of the mounted strangers, thinking man and beast were one. When the Plains Indians eventually stole some horses from the Spanish explorers, they were not sure whether they should eat, ride, or worship them! Once they decided to ride, life changed for the Indians. They became more mobile and could hunt and make war easily.

An old print shows Indian pony with travois.

The costume event is popular at a horse show.

Despite their importance to the tribe, most Indian ponies received no special care. The beasts were frequently scrubby and stunted, due to overwork when they were too young and to poor feeding. Winters were harsh on the prairie and the ponies had hard work to find food. Until the buffalo grass grew in the spring, it was often difficult to see the nobility of their Spanish ancestors in the short, rough bodies.

The Indians did not watch their herds closely and many ponies strayed. Those that escaped formed wild herds and were called *mesteños* (Spanish for strayed) or Mustangs. During Indian raids on other tribes or white settlements, horses often would escape in the confusion. Many of these joined the wild herds thriving on the Great Plains. Numbers increased rapidly. The Indians did not bother these herds—they much preferred to steal already broken mounts from each other.

Cayuse was another name for the Indian pony. Many explorers and settlers had bought ponies from Indians along the trails. Most white men thought that all the Indians they bought from were of the Cayuse tribe. Thus, all ponies were called Cayuse horses. The name stuck, even though many different tribes were represented. Even today, the word Cayuse is synonymous for Indian pony.

Cow Ponies

As the white men moved further and further west, the herds of wild ponies began to get in the way of their settlements. Over the years, hundred of thousands of these wild horses were captured and either killed, driven east to market, or broken for use as cow ponies.

Cattle barons started grazing tremendous herds of cattle where the wild ponies once had roamed. These cattle herds had to be driven long distances to railroads for shipment to market. The only way to do this was with horses. Each cowboy needed from six to ten mounts in a remuda (unit of horses working a cattle drive). The cowboy needed a horse with an

Old print of Texas cow pony at work

Ponies of the Americas are popular in Western events.

inborn cow sense, a horse that could cut a particular animal from the herd, work it to where the rider wanted it, and hold it while it was roped, tied, and branded. During a cattle drive, the cow pony had to "carry his head low and pad along with the steers." No high jinks were allowed near the cattle for fear of stampedes.

The cow pony used for night guard had to be particularly calm, either standing or moving very slowly while the cowboy sang to the herd. It was quickly found that the small, tough, and often ugly Mustangs had this inborn cow sense. Although life was rugged on the cattle drive, the hardy Mustangs thrived on it.

As the cowboy and his horse merged into one glorified being in the eyes of the public, size and looks became important. Easterners began to "breed up" the Mustangs. This may have improved the looks of the little horses but the cow sense was lost. Southwestern ranchers tried crossbreeding with Quarter Horses. This led to the development of the Western cow pony, which was soon in great demand for polo—players reasoned that if a horse could follow a steer it could certainly follow a ball—or for any job requiring speed, stamina, and maneuverability.

Today the Western cow pony is a catch-all type, tracing its descent from nearly every domesticated equine, with particularly large helpings of Quarter Horse added. Often the characteristics and looks of the registered Quarter Horse and the cow pony are so close that it is hard to tell them apart. The modern Western stock horse is actually taller and better looking than its prototypes. Sometimes the only obvious things inherited from the early ancestors are cow sense and the name of cow pony.

The Pony Express

The Pony Express was started in April of 1860 to carry the mail between Missouri and California. Over one thousand horses were used during the nineteen months of its operation. The only ones that could keep up the pace were the hardy little Mustangs, which were not ponies in the technical sense of the word.

Relay stations were set about ten to fifteen miles apart. Horse and rider would cover the distance at a full gallop. Sliding to a stop, the rider would make a lightning switch of mounts and be off again. The tired horse would be rested for a day or two, but the rider went on to cover roughly seventy more miles that day, sometimes through hostile Indian lands.

The completion of the telegraph line signaled the end of the Pony Express in October of 1861 and closed another chapter in the history of the West.

Outrider Ponies

Today at racetracks around the world, the terms "ponies" and "pony boys" are still being used. The pony boy (who nowadays

Horses used at racetracks to assist the start of a race are called ponies whether they are or not.

is often a pony girl), riding a pony, accompanies some racehorses when they leave the stable, either to the exercise track for a workout at some point before the race or to the starting gate for the race itself.

The only requirements for the outrider ponies are steadiness and tractability, while the riders must be strong enough to control their own mounts in addition to the easily excitable racehorses. Famous jockey Ted Atkinson once said, "Sometimes it takes more effort to get a horse to the gate than to race him. That's why so many horses are accompanied to the post by ponies." He explained that the man on the pony uses his strength to keep the racehorse in check so that the jockey does not have to expend his energy until the race actually starts.

Another popular racetrack term is "betting the ponies." Unless one happens to be at a pony-racing track, the saying refers to betting on a horse. Could this term be a hangover from early England when the racing horses were all of pony size?

7 Pony Potpourri

Some ponies, cantering through the ages, have left a mark in history, while others have left a mark only in the lives of their owners. Ponies, whether purebred or grade, have been loved for centuries by everyone from nine to ninety.

One famous mount of long ago documented as pony sized was Bucephalus (meaning ox-head). He was wild and untamable, with a white mark shaped like an ox's head on his own head. When the boy Alexander, son of Philip of Macedonia, saw the fiery black stallion, he begged his father to let him try to ride it. The king was doubtful, but he finally agreed. Alexander controlled Bucephalus, and the two went on to conquer many countries. When Bucephalus died, Alexander, known by then as "the Great," buried him with all the pomp and circumstance due to a hero.

Another famous mount was treated with great respect. The probably pony-sized Incitatus belonged to the mad Roman emperor Caligula. Incitatus was housed in a marble stable with an ivory stall, and he wore a jeweled collar. He was waited on by many slaves, and it was reported that Caligula planned to make him a consul!

Left, *Miss Morgan is a black Morgan pony.* Below, *Before racetracks were built in America, the colonists raced their horses along what roads existed.*

Through the centuries there probably were individual ponies famous in their own countries but there is not much clear evidence, perhaps due to that perplexing question: "What is a pony?"

About the time of the American Revolution, two pony-sized horses lived to become great sires. These, Justin Morgan and Janus, stamped their get with certain characteristics that have been passed consistently from generation to generation.

A pony called Figure was foaled about 1790. Later he was taken to Vermont where he became the property of Justin Morgan, a schoolteacher. He was a bay with black points, standing 14 hands high. There was no task too great for this small horse, and he became famous for the weight he could move in a log-pulling contest. When he died at the old age of thirty, he had sired many foals that inherited his abilities and were renowned for their pulling power. Figure came to be called by his owner's name and was the founder of the breed of horses known as Morgans, many of whom are pony sized today.

Before racetracks became popular in the United States, the pioneers raced their horses over rough tracks, usually a quarter of a mile in length. Horses crossed with the Choctaw and Chickasaw strains were very good at getting off to a flying start and maintaining speed for the quarter-mile sprint. Thoroughbred blood added very little toward the development of this breed, but Janus, an imported English Thoroughbred stallion, was the exception. He and his offspring were well suited to the quarter-mile track. This was probably due to the fact that Janus was shorter than the average Thoroughbred. His name frequently appears in the pedigrees of modern Quarter Horses.

Napoleon had many mounts during his reign in France. It is reputed that he lost sixteen to eighteen horses in the different battles he fought. Most of them were of small stature, as was Napoleon himself. Perhaps the most famous of Bony's mounts was Marengo. This Arabian stallion of 14.1 hands saw Napoleon through many trials.

Fancy was a sorrel gelding about 14 hands high that served on the Confederate side of the War Between the States in America. He belonged to General Stonewall Jackson. Fancy, or Little Sorrel as the soldiers called him, had been purchased by the general for his wife. However, the general found Little Sorrel's gaits so pleasing that he decided to keep him for his own use. The enlisted men grew fond of Little Sorrel and the pony did much to boost the morale of the troops.

Queen Victoria of England enjoyed riding and driving her ponies through the hills of Scotland. These Highland ponies had been chosen for their kind natures and the ability to scramble up over stones without false steps. Victoria's grandson, King George V, carried on the royal fondness for ponies.

The present Queen of England, Elizabeth II, and her children are horse and pony fanciers. When Elizabeth was a child, she and her sister, Princess Margaret, had many ponies. One of the most easily remembered was George, of an indeterminate

65

Old print shows a little girl riding her pony sidesaddle.

breed resembling a Shetland. He came from a coal mine in Durham and proved to be naughty, obstinate, and willful. Among the other royal ponies were a Shetland mare named Peggy and two Welsh ponies, Snowball and Greylight. Queen Elizabeth's first son, Charles, the Prince of Wales, shared Greensleeves and Bandit, Welsh ponies, with his sister, Princess Anne. Their first pony, William, as well as High Jinks, Princess Anne's still loved pony, are both Irish bred. The younger princes, Andrew and Edward, also have had their fair share of ponies to ride and love.

Fubuki, or Silver Tip, came to Japan by the special request of the emperor. Hirohito had long wanted a milk-white Arabian stallion under 15 hands high to carry on a Japanese tradition. When no such pedigreed horse could be found, his agent sent him Silver Tip, an albino cow pony from San Francisco! Hirohito was so delighted with this mount that he accepted him despite the fact that he was not a purebred Arabian.

Peanuts, a very tiny pony, is credited with saving the life of Exterminator, a famous racehorse so bony and lanky that he was nicknamed "Old Bones, the Galloping Hatrack." When Exterminator was retired from the racetrack and put to pasture, he was so lonesome his owners feared he might die. So Peanuts was put out to join him, and the two got along fine. Unfortunately, Peanuts died soon afterward, so a Peanuts II had to be found. Everyone hoped that Exterminator would accept the replacement, and when he did, sighs of relief were heard. It was quite a sight to see the two friends; the tiny pony running under the rangy racer's belly.

Two recent famous jumping ponies are Little Squire (First Attempt) and Stroller. Little Squire was a Connemara and the

Marion Coakes on Stroller, by Sam Savitt

wizard of the Irish Army Team. He was the first pony ever named champion jumper at Madison Square Garden (1939). He could clear 6'6" with a bareback rider, and 7' riderless. At shows, a single six-foot-high pole would be set up in exhibition. Little Squire would be ridden under it, then turned around and jumped over it to show his remarkable ability!

Stroller was on the British Equestrian Team in the 1960's and was a phenomenal jumper. Ridden by Marion Coakes, Stroller won awards and ribbons in many different countries, including a silver medal in the 1968 Olympics in Mexico. It was a special thrill at horse shows to see the little bay, classified as a pony, flying over jumps that towered above him.

8 Uses of Ponies

Since the domestication of horses and ponies, there is hardly an area of man's life that has not been affected by them. There is truth in the well-known quotation: "Wherever man has left his footprint in the long ascent from barbarism to civilization, we will find the hoofprint of the horse beside it."

The first and simplest way horses and ponies served man was to provide a source of food and clothing. Primitive man was a hunter and a forager, forced to lead a nomadic life following game and harvests. Cave paintings, such as those found in Lascaux, France, depict how man hunted ponies for food and skins. Bones, also found in caves, give silent testimony to the use made of ponies in prehistoric times.

The exact date of the domestication of the horse or pony is unclear. Man, the hunter, eventually found that the pony's strongest and most important characteristic was its ability to run. Once this was established, ponies became too valuable to be eaten, and man began to discover other uses for them. The ancient Mesopotamians called the horse *asva*, the Sanskrit for swiftness, while the word *equus* is taken from the Latin *acer*, meaning quickness.

Strong evidence points to the Chinese as the first to harness and drive ponies, and also to ride them. Harness, used for draft work, was invented by them somewhere about 4000-3000 B.C. During the same millenium, the Assyrians and the Persians became skilled riders. The Assyrians were the first to have a cavalry. Stone tablets engraved in 1400 B.C. in Asia Minor show a day-to-day record of the selection, care, and training of horses. As noted, polo was being played by 600 B.C. The Greeks were using their ponies to pull war chariots as well as for riding about 350 B.C.

When Julius Caesar invaded Britain in 55-54 B.C., he was impressed with the skill of the British charioteers. They had their ponies trained to pull chariots at a full gallop, then check and turn all in a moment. Pieces of harness still in existence show that these ponies were about 12 hands high. A British commander, Cassivellaunus, was said to have had four thousand chariots. He led the resistance to Caesar's second invasion, using his charioteers and guerrilla tactics.

Maximum Usefulness

Ponies continued to serve man in various ways through all the centuries. They hit their peak of usefulness during the years 1600-1900. During these times ponies were used for making war, for hunting, agriculture, and for sport. Perhaps the most important area of their service was transportation of goods and people, in harness as well as not.

Beasts of Burden

Palfreys and pack ponies were the chief beasts of burden used for transporting men and goods from the seventeenth through the nineteenth centuries.

A palfrey was a quiet saddle horse, or pony, about 14 hands

The ponies of England have been used in all types of work for centuries. These are Dartmoor ponies in Devon.

high, popular for its even pacing motion. Ladies were very fond of palfries because they made such good mounts, able to travel for miles at a comfortable stride.

Pack ponies were responsible for the transportation of every kind of goods imaginable. Each sturdy little beast could carry many times its weight and often walk more than two hundred miles a week, while surviving on minimum food. Mounted men shepherded the ponies along in long trains from one town or village to another. Often these trains would tie up traffic for miles in either direction because the roads were so poor and narrow. Peddlers and traders also used ponies to carry their wares from house to house.

While most pack ponies were put to legitimate work, others

were used by smugglers and robbers. Smuggling was best done on dark and stormy nights, especially along coastlines. Imagine the poor ponies with their feet, and often their heads, muffled so no noise would betray the thieves. The ponies were often drenched with rain or sleet, as well as spray from the ocean, as they labored to deliver the illegal "whiskey for the parson, brandy for the clerk."

After a while people began to realize that trains of pack ponies were impractical and costly. Gradually inland waterway systems were developed, roads were improved, and larger horses began to be useful for towing barges or pulling heavy wagons. Although pack ponies still would continue to be used in remote hilly areas and by the lone peddlar, tinker, or trader, the day of large trains of pack ponies was over. Therefore breeders and owners began to look toward other tasks for which their diminutive beasts of burden were suited.

In the Traces

Ponies in harness played an important role in the mining history of England. In 1842, Great Britain passed a Mines Act which forbade underground employment of women or of boys under ten. Ponies quickly became a cash crop as replacements for the people in the mines. The smaller the pony the more valuable, so breeders started breeding down for size. At one point there were about 100,000 ponies working in the coal mines of Britain. The ponies, mostly male, could cover about thirty miles a day pulling carts of coal. Rumors of terrible working conditions, poor feeding, accidents, and blindness abounded. Many of the ponies spent their entire lives below ground.

A Coal Mines Regulation Act was passed in 1887 in an attempt to protect the ponies, but mine owners would not let inspectors enter the mines. In 1914, the Society for the Protection of Pit Ponies was founded. The changes it strove for could not become reality until the methods of production were changed. Mechanization of mines during the 1930's released many thousands of ponies, and stricter laws have improved conditions to the point that pit ponies were found to live longer—sometimes to twenty-five years. In 1962 only approximately six thousand ponies still worked in British mines, although this was a greater number than in any other western European country.

Pony driving and racing were both very popular in the United States and England in the seventeenth through nineteenth centuries and up until the the first World War. Many people owned carts and wagons for picnics, afternoon rides, or doing odd jobs. The primary gait of these ponies was a trot.

Twentieth-century Usefulness

Today in many areas of the world ponies still continue to serve traditional roles. In remote and hilly sections they may be the sole method of transportation, both of goods and people. Shooting ponies still carry the day's game home in Scotland and England, while travelers to the Himalayas find themselves riding up and down the narrow mountain trails on small hill ponies—ponies that are also used to carry packs over these same trails. To avoid bumping their packs against the side of the mountain, the ponies have developed the habit of always walking close to the outer edge of the path, no matter what their burden. This habit can be extremely nerve wracking to the newly arrived traveler!

Ponies are still used for farming in many countries. In the British Isles, they haul peat, a traditional source of fuel cut from the bogs. In the city of London are many "coster" ponies which still take goods to and from the borough markets, as well as on established routes. Butchers used coster ponies until the beginning of the twentieth century. An errand boy would be sent out each morning to get the meat orders from the cooks along his route. He would then return to the shop, and when the order was filled he would deliver it back to the cook in time for her to prepare the meat for dinner. All this had to be done with the pony at the trot, because faster gaits were forbidden in the cities of England and on the Continent. Because dinner then was much earlier and more elaborate than it is today, the butcher boy and his coster pony had to be abroad in the wee hours of the dawn.

To the Ends of the Earth

It can truthfully be said that ponies have been all over the world. In addition to having crossed the land bridge several times in antiquity, in modern times they have been to the Arctic and the Antarctic. Ernest Shackleton was the first to take ponies to Antarctica, along with dogs and the first automobile to reach that continent. But the experiment with the car was not successful, and while Shackleton was enthusiastic about the ponies' performance, misfortune overtook the expedition and the goal of the South Pole was not reached.

Some years later Robert Scott depended on ponies as his primary means of transport to the Pole. Although Scott and his companions gained the Pole, they lost their lives on the return trip. All the ponies that went on the two expeditions died too, either from accidents or because they were shot for food when their usefulness as beasts of burden came to an end. But they had played an integral part in the early explorations of the seventh continent. Since then, no horses have been used at the South Pole because of the extreme weather conditions there. Planes and helicopters now transport workers and visitors to the remote stations of Antarctica.

Some of the ponies from Shackleton's expedition

UNDER THE BIG TOP

Besides their traditional role of transporting goods and persons, ponies continue to serve man in other areas. Circus ponies have been a delight to everyone for ages and will no doubt continue to amuse and enchant audiences as long as there is a Big Top. Whether the pony acts as the "Joey," the clown's pony, and performs daring antics such as stealing his handkerchief, butting the ringmaster, or charging the other clowns, or whether it performs the controlled movements of a Liberty Horse, it invariably charms and captivates the crowds.

A calm and trustworthy disposition is as necessary to the acrobat's circus pony as the pony is to the athlete, because timing must be exact. This sense of timing is also important when the pony works with other circus animals. It is reputed that Ringling Brothers Circus at one time had a draft horse and a tiny Shetland with exactly the same color and markings. At

Ponies are in demand for trail rides and shows. Pride of Tennessee, above, a six-year-old Tennessee Walking Horse pony, is comfortable to ride, in or out of shows.

A lonesome dappled gray, left, waits for a trail ride.

Candy Cane, below, a Welsh pony, has a flaxen mane and tail.

one point in the act, the draft horse would go to the middle of the ring while the pony ran figure eights around and under him. This was to show the difference in size as well as the importance of timing.

Pony Clubs in Britain

In Great Britain there was a revival of interest in ponies soon after World War I. The British Pony Clubs were incorporated in 1928 and started to run instructional and competitive events for children with or without their own ponies. This was an ideal opportunity for many youngsters to learn how to care for ponies, ride and work with them, and compete in shows and activities. Within three years there were over one hundred branches. Today the Pony Clubs are stronger and more active than ever and have spread to other countries.

The Ponies of Britain Club was formed in 1952. This was done when it was discovered that many British ponies were being sold for meat and that some breeds were in danger of becoming extinct. The work of this club has stopped much of the practice of selling ponies to slaughterhouses.

Pony Trekking

Trekking has been instrumental in the return of interest in the pony. The word *trek* is from the Afrikaans and used to mean journey, march, or migration by ox wagons or cape carts. Today in the British Isles as well as elsewhere trekking is actually quite different.

The trek, or ride, will start from a stable or center and take a lengthy trip along a previously marked route. The trek is conducted mostly at a walk, and lunch is eaten on the way. Often the trekkers will camp out for one or several nights. Trekking is loved by all who participate, both for the exercise and for the chance to be out of doors with horses.

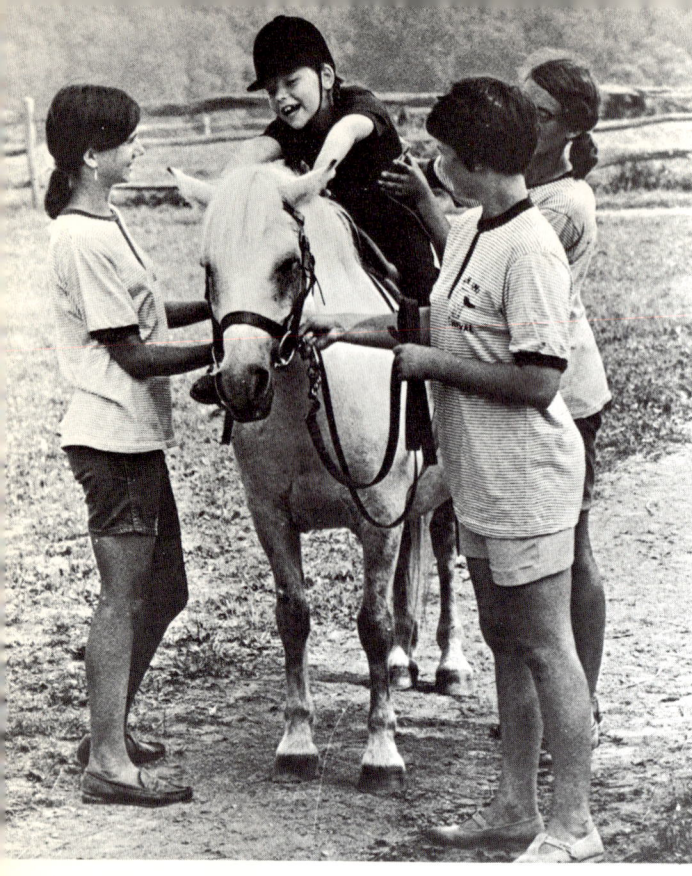

Docile, kind-natured ponies are invaluable in therapy and for handicapped riders' clubs all over the world.

PONIES IN THE UNITED STATES

It wasn't until after World War II that there was a revived interest in ponies in the United States. In 1954, United States Pony Clubs, Inc., was founded. Today there is an increase in places where one can rent ponies for all day or overnight rides, although this is not called trekking. Driving ponies, as well as racing them, has undergone an upsurge in popularity in America. There is a trend, too, toward breeding fine animals suited for the show ring.

PONIES FOR THERAPY

Recently it was discovered that riding has great therapeutic value for the handicapped. In 1947 there was a widespread polio epidemic in England and Norway. Severely disabled children who were still recuperating performed exercises on horseback with great results. Liz Hartnell provided a source of inspiration. Although she was paralyzed by polio, she became an Olympic dressage rider. One enthusiastic supporter of the Canadian Association for Riding for the Disabled (C.A.R.D.) said recently, "Many times I have been reduced to tears to see the eyes of a crippled child brighten with love for his pony as he tried to pat it in appreciation for the ride."

In addition to Canada, ponies are being used all over the world today as part of the therapy for crippled, limbless, autistic, mentally retarded, or emotionally disturbed people. Happy Horsemanship for Handicapped, Inc., is a national organization in the United States.

In spite of the many present-day uses of ponies, man is no longer as dependent on equines as he once was. Nevertheless, the mystique that surrounds horses and ponies will never fade, as long as there are boys and girls to love and ride them. The evidence is strong that as man continues to leave his footprints in time, close beside will be found the hoofprint of the horse as well as the tinier one of the pony.

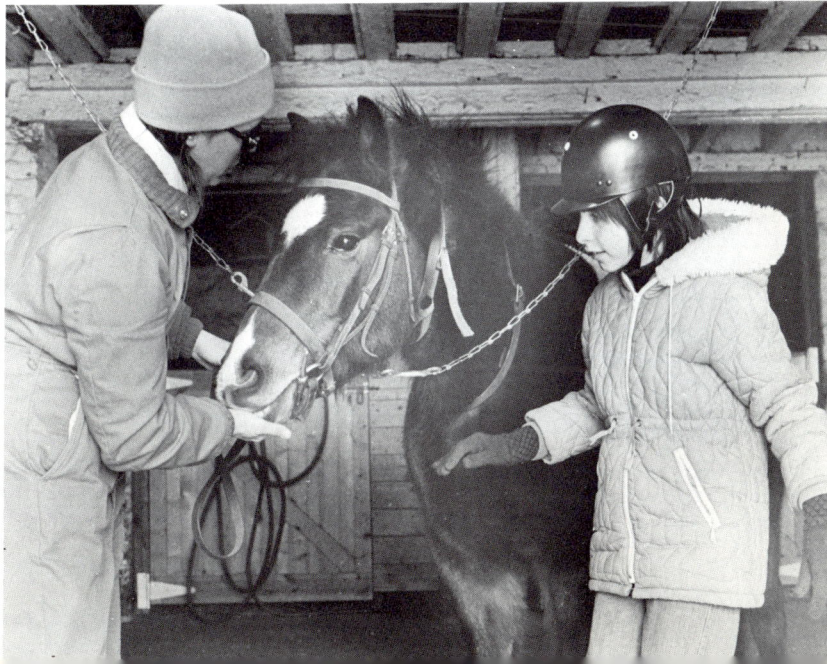

Index

Alexander, 63
Assateague Island, 43–45, 55
Atkinson, Ted, 62

Batak pony, 25

Caligula, 63
Canadian Association for Riding for the Disabled (C.A.R.D.), 79
Canute, King, 37
Cassivellaunus, 70
Cayuse, 58–59
Celtic pony, 22, 24, 27, 46
Chincoteague pony, 43–45
Coakes, Marion, 68
Connemara pony, 28–31, 67
Cow ponies, 59–61

Dales pony, 37–38
Dartmoor pony, 34, 35–36

Elizabeth II, Queen, 65
Exmoor pony, 34–35
Exterminator, 67

Face markings, 17
Falabella pony, 41–42
Fancy, 65
Fell pony, 37–38
Folklore, 51–52
Fubuki, 66–67

George V, King, 65
Griffins, 57

Hackney pony, 45–46
Haflinger pony, 42–43
Happy Horsemanship for Handicapped, Inc., 79
Hartwell, Liz, 70
Hirohito, Emperor, 66
Horse, history of, 18–24
    Appaloosa, 39, 40, 41
    Arabian, 32, 36, 39, 40, 42, 54, 65
    Clydesdale, 20
    Frisian, 38
    Hackney, 32, 33
    Percheron, 20
    Przewalsky's, 20–21
    Quarter, 8, 39, 40, 60, 61
    Spanish, 29
    Tarpan, 21–22
    Thoroughbred, 8, 32–33, 36, 65

Icelandic pony, 46–48

Incitatus, 63
Indian ponies, 43, 57–59

Jackson, Gen. Stonewall, 65
Janus, 64, 65
Julius Caesar, 24, 32, 70

Kathiawari pony, 25

Little Squire, 67–68

Manipur pony, 25
Marengo, 65
Mongolian pony, 56–57
Morgan, Justin, 64
Mustang, 58, 60–61
Mythology, 49–51

Napoleon, 65
New Forest pony, 36–37
Nez Percé Indians, 12

Outrider ponies, 61–62

Pindos pony, 25
"Points," 12
Polo ponies, 56–57, 60–61
Ponies
    ancestry of, 22, 49
    characteristics, 10–17. *See also* individual breeds.
    definition of, 7–9
    grade, 9
    lore about, 49–55
    purebred, 9
    uses of, 9, 69–74
Ponies of Britain Club, 75
Pony clubs, 77, 78
Pony Express, 61
Pony of the Americas, 39–40
Pony Penning Day, 44

Scott, Robert, 74
Shackleton, Ernest, 74
Shetland pony, 22, 25–27, 39, 41, 44, 67
Society for the Protection of Pit Ponies, 73
Stroller, 68

Therapy, ponies for, 78–79
Trekking, 77

Victoria, Queen, 65

Welsh cob, 29
Welsh Mountain pony, 32
Welsh pony, 32

J636.1   336981
Lavine
Wonders of ponies.

Johnson Free Public Library

Hackensack, New Jersey